• Bartholomew •

Best Walks
IN THE
LAKE DISTRICT

by John Parker

Bartholomew
An Imprint of HarperCollins*Publishers*

CONTENTS

A Bartholomew Walk Guide
Published by Bartholomew
An Imprint of HarperCollins*Publishers*
77-85 Fulham Palace Road
London W6 8JB

First published 1996
Text © John Parker 1996
Maps © Bartholomew 1996

The walks contained in this guide were first published in Bartholomew's Walk the Lakes

Printed in Great Britain by Scotprint Limited, Musselburgh

ISBN 0 7028 3518 8
96/1/16

All rights reserved. No part of this publication may be reproduced, stored in a retrieval system, or transmitted in any form or by any means, electronic, mechanical, photocopying, recording, or otherwise, without the prior permission of the Publisher.

The landscape is changing all the time. While every care has been taken in the preparation of this guide, the Publisher accepts no responsibility whatsoever for any loss, damage, injury or inconvenience sustained or caused as a result of using this guide.

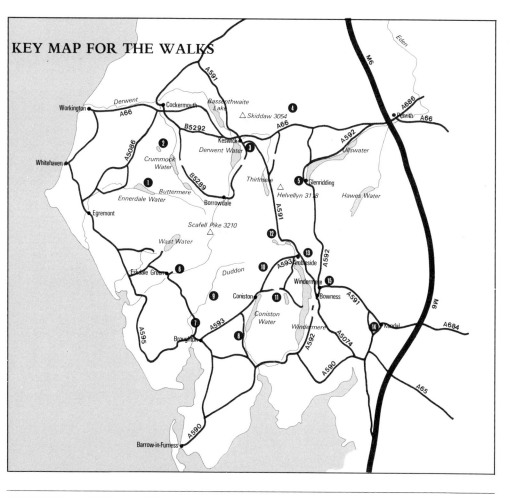

KEY MAP FOR THE WALKS

Workington • Derwent • Cockermouth • Bassenthwaite Lake • △ Skiddaw 3054 • Penrith • Eden • M6 • A591 • A66 • A686 • A66 • B5292 • A592

Whitehaven • A5086 • **2** • Crummock Water • Keswick • **3** • Derwent Water • Ullswater

1 • Buttermere • Ennerdale Water • Borrowdale • B5289 • Thirlmere • △ Helvellyn 3118 • **5** Glenridding • Hawes Water

Egremont • Scafell Pike 3210 △ • Wast Water • Duddon • **12** • **13** Ambleside • A593 • A592

Eskdale Green • **6** • **10** • Windermere • **15** Bowness • A591

9 • Coniston • **11** • Coniston Water • Windermere

7 • A593 • Broughton • **8** • A592 • A5074 • **14** Kendal • A684 • M6

A595 • A590 • A65

Barrow-in-Furness •

KEY TO SCALE AND MAP SYMBOLS

SCALE 1:63 360

miles
0   1   2   3   4   5
0 1 2 3 4 5 6 7 8
kilometres

- - - - Route of Walk   ═══ Road   · 547 Spot height in feet
⑨ - Walking directions   ::::: Other tracks and footpaths   ♣ Site of antiquity
Ⓔ - Description of viewpoint   Y.H. ▲ Youth hostel   ⓘ Information Centre

| 0 | 152 | 213 | 305 | 610 | 686 | 762 | 914 | Metres |
| 0 | 500 | 700 | 1000 | 2000 | 2250 | 2500 | 3000 | Feet |

3

INTRODUCTION

1 ON THE REAL ART OF WALKING

Some walkers revel in mileage. Some collect long-distance footpaths like other people collect stamps, while others run around many miles in wild country on map-reading races. Some would point to the need of modern spoon-fed society to tax sloppy muscles once in a while. But is there not also another, perhaps greater, need? True recreation is a re-creation. In the natural beauty of the countryside one can find an oasis of reassurance in that confusing desert of changing modern values. It is a 'going back' to the beginning. The true art of walking consists not of packing distance into moments, but of packing enjoyable moments into distance.

Who enjoys vintage wine by gulping draughts of it? It must be held on the palate and savoured slowly. Many, perhaps, could easily knock off four of the walks described here in one day. That would be foolish when there is so much to savour in each one. What this book does is point to a few features on these selected walks and leaves the rest for discovery. What is left to the walker is his or her awareness.

It must be recognised, however, that in the normal human state, awareness is dulled. Overwhelmed by the sensations pouring in at us from all sides, we habitually filter them out and accept only what we want and think we need. We receive only what we are 'tuned in' to receive. It could be as our own Lake District bard, William Wordsworth, said:

'The world is too much with us;
   late and soon,
Getting and spending we lay waste
   our powers:
Little we see in nature that is ours;
We have given our hearts away, ...' (1).

But all is not lost if we realise that these limitations are self-inflicted. All we have to do is to awaken our senses and willingly accept nature's messages in sight, scent and sound. That means complete relaxation in freedom. There is no need to accept the tyranny of a distance walking programme; no need to look on the Lake District as some vast open air gymnasium. Distance and muscle straining is not the objective here. What we look for in these walks is not quantity, but quality.

'Ah', some might say, 'but the best views are from the mountain tops'. That is nonsense. The best views surely consist of the two extreme elements juxtaposed; the active and the passive. Mountains and lake, or the frozen violence of steep crags set above the green calm of the dale. It is true that John Ruskin (1819-1900), the supreme arbiter of good taste in scenery said 'Mountains are the beginning and the end of all natural scenery.' (2) He spent his last 25 years in contemplating them from the supreme low-level viewpoint of his Coniston lakeside house. A high viewpoint is not necessary; a low one is often just as good and indeed can be better.

The pleasures of these walks can be shared by any reasonably active family, which is why they were chosen. Beyond modest physical effort and a minimum of equipment, all that is needed is that 'eye to perceive, and a heart to enjoy' (3).

References

(1) Wordsworth W. The World is too much with us. *Miscellaneous Sonnets*. Part 1; XXXlll.

(2) Ruskin J. *Modern Painters*. London, 1888. Vol IV; Part V: Chapter 20.

(3) Wordsworth W. *Guide to the Lakes*. London 1835.

2 WHAT EQUIPMENT?

For ordinary fell walking it is not necessary to purchase expensive equipment as though you were about to tackle the north face of the Eiger. It is bad logic to assume that, for instance, a pair of boots good enough for scaling the Alps must be good enough for Loughrigg Fell. Ice and snow are not the norm here. Footwear should be reasonably strong, not too heavy and preferably worn over wool socks or stockings. Nylon can give blisters. Soles of the boots should be cleated or wedged, rather than smooth. Sliding around wastes a lot of energy and can lead to falls and broken bones as easily as a fall of several feet. Boots should grip neatly and comfortably round the ankle so preventing the feet moving and rubbing into blisters. To summarise; boots should be strong, light, comfortable and provide grip.

Clothing too should be comfortable. As it can rain hard in the Lake District it is advisable to carry a light rucksack with a light waterproof and if possible waterproof trousers too. These should protect you from the worst of the weather unless you are walking in the depths of winter, when more specialist clothing is likely to be necessary.

Carrying a rucksack leaves the hands and arms free. If walking as a family, the loads can be shared. It is always advisable to carry something to eat as walks can take longer than anticipated, especially if one lingers at a particularly pleasant viewpoint or quiet corner. A basic first aid kit with a few self-adhesive dressings for possible blisters and cuts, and an ointment for insect bites should be carried. In mid-summer it is a good idea to take along a proprietary brand of insect repellent.

An one inch to the mile (1:63 360) or metric (1:50 000) map, as well as this guide book, is useful for putting the walk into context and for identifying the distant terrain.

3 PUBLIC RIGHTS OF WAY

There is more freedom to walk in the Lake District than possibly anywhere else in Britain. On offer there is everything, from easy walks by lake shores to rough scrambles on the high fells. The fells are open to all, not by right, but by traditional let. But it should be clear that though the Lake District is a National Park that does not mean that all the land belongs to the nation. Most of the land is privately owned, and farmed or grazed, and much of the valley land is enclosed. However, a vast network of public rights of way through this private land means that little is denied to the walker. With a map the rights of way can be identified; they are marked in red on the one inch (1:63 360) map; public footpaths as red dots and bridleways as dashes.

The *National Parks and Access to the Countryside Act* 1949 tidied up the law on rights of way. Following the process of public consultation, maps were drawn by the County Authorities of England and Wales showing all the rights of way. Copies of the definitive maps are available for public inspection. Once on the map the right of way becomes irrefutable.

What the right means

Any member of the public can pass freely on a public right of way, on foot, on a footpath, on horseback or cycle on a bridleway. No one can lawfully interfere with that right; not even the landowner. It would be wrong, for instance, for a landowner to move anyone away with the argument that the definitive map was wrongly drawn. It may be so, but until the error is lawfully corrected by the prescribed process the path remains a public thoroughfare.

The walker has the right to pass along the right of way and rest on it for a reasonable length of time. He has no right, for instance, to take a deck chair, a radio and a picnic basket and sunbathe on it! The landowner or his tenant must not obstruct the right of passage in any way. He must maintain the stiles and gates on the path so as to offer unrestricted passage, a duty which seems rather unfair on him, though he can obtain help in meeting the maintenance costs from the Highways Authority. The landowner must not erect any notice which might discourage, or lead the public to believe that a right of way does not exist.

A member of the public has the right to remove any obstruction which he might encounter on the route. He has, however, no right to go purposely onto a right of way, knowing it to be obstructed, with the intention of removing the obstruction. It is required that any report of a known obstruction should be communicated to the Highways Authority (in the case of the Lake District to the Lake District Special Planning Board, Busher Walk, Kendal) who can compel the owner to remove the obstruction, or can remove it and charge the landowner with the cost of doing so.

A walker can take his dog with him on a public right of way so long as it is under close control. A farmer has the right to shoot a dog which is worrying, or he has reason to suspect is about to worry, sheep. Under the *Wildlife and Countryside Act* 1982 it is even an offense to have a dog not under close control in a field containing sheep; the dog owner can be fined heavily. Under the same Act a farmer can put a mature bull into a field crossed by a right of way so long as it is a beef bull, which is usually more docile; cows must be present too. How the ordinary walker can tell one bull breed from another is not clear. If it is a black and white Friesian, which is a dairy bull, it is illegal and definitely to be avoided!

No one can drive any vehicle, including a motorcycle, along a public footpath or bridleway unless he has the landowner's consent. It would be wrong to assume every motor cyclist on a public path is offending. Some shepherds now use motorcycles to get to, and to round up sheep.

The Highways Authority has the responsibility of maintaining rights of way, and the bridges on it, in reasonable condition. That does not mean, of course, that it should pave them all or do anything beyond ensuring that the users are not unduly impeded by extreme wear and tear. The Authority has the duty to place, with the consent of the Parish Councils concerned, footpath signs at the points where public rights of way leave public highways. However, it could take many years, at the present rate of progress, before this duty is completed. The Authority can also waymark paths, and erect further sign posts on the route, if necessary.

The responsibilities

Rights usually carry responsibilities and these are a matter of reasonable commonsense. 'The rights of the individuals should be thus far limited' said John Stuart Mill, 'that he must not be a nuisance to other people.' If a walker must pass through a closed gate on his route, naturally he should close it behind him. If there is a group of walkers, the rule should be not more than two abreast across paths on farm fields. Every square yard (or metre) of grass is vital to the farmer.

4   A CODE FOR COUNTRYGOERS

No countrygoer should ever drop litter. Everyone knows this but it bears repeating for the National Park authority, and the National Trust, using hard-pressed staff and volunteers, have to make constant costly efforts to remove the mess left by unthinking people. The fact that a footpath is clean does not mean, alas, that all walkers are respecting the countryside. It could mean that a group of volunteers has just cleaned it. It is no trouble to pocket litter until it can be disposed of correctly.

Obviously flowers and plants encountered on a walk should not be taken but left for others passing to enjoy. To use the excuse 'I have only taken a few' is futile. If everyone only took a few the country would be devastated. If young wild animals are encountered they should be left well alone. For instance, although they might not often be seen in full daylight, deer, both roe and red, are common in the Lake District. If a fawn or a deer calf is discovered lying still in the grass it would be wrong to assume that it has been abandoned.

Mothers hide their offspring while they go away to graze and browse and return to them at feeding time. If the animals are touched it could mean that they will be abandoned as the human scent might deter the mother from returning to her offspring. Similarly with baby birds, who have not yet mastered flight; they may appear to have been abandoned but often are being watched by their parents who might be waiting for a walker to pass on before coming out to give flight lesson two!

What appear to be harmful snakes should not be killed because firstly the 'snake' could well be a slow worm, which looks like a snake but is really a harmless legless lizard, and second, even if it were an adder (they are quite common) it will escape if given the opportunity. Adders are part of the pattern of nature and should not be persecuted. They rarely bite unless they are handled; a foolish act, which is not uncommon; or stood on, which is rare, as the snakes are usually basking in full view and are quick to escape. Adder bites are rarely serious and panic is quite unnecessary.

For his or her own safety a walker should take care when walking on country roads. The advice usually given is to walk on the right so as to face oncoming traffic, but sometimes this can be dangerous. The rule should be qualified with the advice that the outside should be taken on blind bends so that traffic in both directions can see the walker.

Countrygoers should take care not to start fires. The danger time in the Lake District is usually in a dry spring when the previous year's bracken and undergrowth is tinder dry. A carelessly discarded cigarette end can cause thousands of pounds worth of damage.

Lastly, remote homes and communities depend on fell side becks and pools for their water supplies, even when the Water Authority's huge extraction plants are close at hand. Everyone should be quite sure before bathing that the tempting pools or becks are not someone's supply. Ask first!

When walking over enclosed land it is necessary to read your map accurately so as to avoid trespassing and damage to walls by crossing at the wrong place; a frequent cause for complaint. The stiles and gates provided should *always* be used.

5   MAP READING

A map is a representation, on flat paper, of the three-dimensional features of the earth. Some boast that given an one inch to the mile

(1:63 360) or metric (1:50 000) map of some strange country they can scan a part of it, and have a mental picture of the landscape it represents. This is possibly an exaggeration. The map certainly details the bones of the landscape; the flesh is left to the imagination. As a map has severe spatial and dimensional limitations, it is necessary to interpret. This needs practice. Usually a family walking party has one good map reader and that task is left to him or her. This is unwise; everyone should have a turn! Map reading is important as it is the key to enjoying the countryside. Anyone who lacks this easily acquired skill is denied an essential freedom.

The map's key and the scale are detailed at its base. A brief study is necessary. Once the key features of roads, footpaths, watercourses and hills have been learned you should not get lost. One of the most common mistakes to make when map reading is the wrong identification of the point where you are standing. The path or road is identifiable but the precise place is not. The problem can be solved by correct orientation of the map; that is place the map so that the top is towards the north. The easiest way to do this is to place a compass on it with the north point on the compass card pointing to the top. The map, compass card and the map reader (if he is to avoid reading it sideways or upside down) should all be turned until the compass needle points to the magnetic north, which is currently six degrees to the west of north (354 degrees on the scale). Once the map is orientated, some of the visible physical features can be identified and then with the aid of the map your position in relation to them fixed. Another way to orientate a map without a compass is to turn it until some identifiable feature in the landscape (a church for example) is lined up with the map, then all the other features should fit into place.

Orientation is particularly useful at a viewpoint when you are trying to identify distant features, such as hills or mountain peaks.

Excusably, one can regard the need to watch the time as tyranny when walking for pleasure. However, a watch is also a useful tool when map reading. For example, if you knew that it was 1100 hours when you were standing at the tarn and you know that your family walks about two miles (three km) per hour on a reasonably level route and that it is now 1130 hours, then on the one inch to the mile (1:63 360) map you should fix yourself about one inch (2.5 cm) from the tarn. This, of course, assumes level ground. The other features on the map which one must master, are the contours. Experience might prove that you need to take account in your calculations of the need to add five minutes to every 100 feet (30.5m) of climbing, which is fairly average for a family. So if the journey from the tarn involved a 100 feet (30.5m) of climb as you see it from the interpretation of the contours and a glance back at the terrain, that takes five minutes (1/6 inches or 4mm) off your distance on the map.

With this formula you can estimate the time it will take to do one of the walks in this book, but to the walking time one has to add talking time, not to mention the looking, photographing, eating and sunbathing, and the luxurious idleness time. All this might be something of a challenge to map readers, but the exercise can be entertaining and the experience in the long run invaluable! However, good map reading still requires lots of practice.

6 SOME PRECAUTIONARY NOTES – SAFETY

The walks in this book have been chosen with safety as well as enjoyment in mind. However accidents can happen even in the easiest terrain and 90 per cent of these can be avoided. There are the obvious precautions of keeping children away from quarry and rock faces, holes and unstable river banks. The falls which happen are usually caused by poor, particularly smooth-soled, footwear. What might be suitable for the town is a liability in the country. A fall can also be caused by the bad placing of feet, almost always *on the descent*. This usually happens when someone is in a hurry or is losing concentration from tiredness. Boisterous children must be restrained from running downhill. It is absolutely vital to look at where you are about to place your feet. Remember dry steep grass, or wet grass, can be as slippy as the other more obvious hazard of smooth wet rock. Tripping is another cause of falls. Watchfulness is again the answer. Accident records for walkers in the Lake District show a surprising number which have been caused by tripping over a dog lead!

Bogs in the vicinity of these walks are not generally considered to be a danger, but can cause some discomfort! Beware of ground which is bright green, or grey-green with sphagnum moss. If you find yourself bogged down, make for the bracken or heather, neither of which can grow on bog.

Even the most careful can sometimes sprain an ankle. Should an accident happen to a member of the family and you are near enough the road to help yourself, then you or someone else should try to get to a telephone. Dial 999 and ask for Police and Mountain Rescue; give accurate details of location and, if possible, the injury. That is all that is necessary at that stage. If it is your practice to walk alone, then the most obvious precaution for you to take is to leave route details with someone at 'base'. This seems elementary, but there have been many occasions on which someone has not returned from a walk and no one else has any idea where that person intended to go. A search party has then to rely on guesswork; that could mean many expensive man-hours, or days before the casualty is found. If you leave the details, a search party has a better idea, at least, of where to look.

Lastly, safety of property; some of these walks start from quiet unobserved areas where thieves can be undisturbed. It is not a good idea to leave the car unlocked or valuables on display in it. Lock everything in the boot.

7   THE NATIONAL PARK AND THE NATIONAL TRUST

The Lake District was already attracting great numbers of tourists before Wordsworth wrote his famous *Guide to the Lakes* in the first half of last century, and the wealthy were also buying tracts of prime scenic countryside on which to build their own country seats. Wordsworth in his Guide's concluding chapter expresses a hope that 'better taste should prevail' and adds: 'In this wish the author will be joined by persons of pure taste throughout the whole island, who, by their visits (often repeated) to the Lakes in the North of England, testify that they deem the district a sort of national property, in which every man has a right and interest who has an eye to perceive and a heart to enjoy.' Since that time there have been changes that Wordsworth would have deplored, but his wish has received a good deal of sympathetic, if somewhat tardy, response. The world's first National Park was born at Yellowstone in the United States in 1872. The first practical moves in conservation in Britain came much later and took a rather different, perhaps typically British, shape.

The National Trust

Late in the 19th century the incumbent at Crosthwaite church in Keswick was one Canon Hardwicke Rawnsley, an extraordinarily energetic man; poet, traveller, athlete, historian, preacher and campaigner, as well as passionate lover of the Lake District. In 1890 a parishioner told him that he had been compelled to buy some land from his neighbour to prevent his felling some fine trees. Rawnsley accepted the idea that the purchase of property was the only sure way to preserve it, and he was concerned about the growing threats to unspoilt country and historical sites. With the supporting efforts of another great campaigner and reformer, Octavia Hill and another friend, Robert Hunter, Solicitor to the Post office, an organisation was founded which sought to acquire and preserve property, by gift or purchase by public subscription. It was thus that the National Trust, a charity, was officially launched in 1895.

Some of the Trust's first acquisitions were in Rawnsley's own area. In 1902 Brandelhow, on the west side of Derwentwater, was bought by public subscription. Nearby Manesty Park was bought in 1908 before it could be parcelled up into building plots. Over the years since large areas of the Lake District have come into the care of the National Trust. Notable benefactors have included Dr George Trevelyan, the historian who gave properties in Langdale, and artist/author Beatrix Potter, who as a girl had met Canon Rawnsley. Thanks to her the Trust gained some 4000 acres (1620ha) and 14 farms. Now the National Trust is the largest landowner in the Lake District and has made it possible for traditional farming to continue in many dales, and vast areas of broadleaf woodlands to be protected.

The National Park

The Lake District National Park is the largest of the National Parks in England and Wales, with 866 square miles (2242sq.km). The Act which established National Parks came into being 140 years after Wordsworth's expression of concern, and 77 years after Yellowstone. The first strongly organised pressure for National Parks and access to mountains came during the 1920s and 1930s when walking and mountaineering became popular pastimes and access to open country in some parts of Britain was much restricted. The outbreak of war postponed progress, and following the reports of John

Dower on the need, and the Hobhouse committee's recommendations on implementation, an Act, The *National Parks and Access to the Countryside Act* 1949, was passed. 'People need the refreshment which is obtainable from the beauty and quietness of unspoilt country.' The provision for those needs of the people and the protection from spoilation, were written into the Act.

In many countries of the world National Parks are areas of wilderness hardly influenced by man, and the land of these parks is owned by the nation or state. There is no true wilderness left in Britain. The natural beauty of the landscape reflects the pattern of husbandry, and with so many owning and making a living from the land nationalisation of it was not contemplated. A British National Park is a defined area of unspoilt countryside, usually with some wild, if not wilderness country, specially protected from unsuitable development; public access for its enjoyment is secured, and due regard made for the needs of the local community.

The National Park authority must exercise planning control, but must also provide information and ranger services. In the Lake District the authority also owns a visitor centre at Brockhole, Windermere, and has responsibility for the maintenance of public footpaths and bridleways. It also owns extensive areas of hill commonland, woodland and lake.

The National Trust, the charity, and the National Park, the local government authority, work closely with other large landowners, the Forestry Commission and the Water Authority, to provide protected public access unrivalled anywhere else in Britain. It is indeed as Wordsworth said 'a sort of national property' for those 'with eyes to perceive and hearts to enjoy.'

Addresses

The National Trust
National Trust Regional Office
The Hollens
Grasmere, Ambleside LA22 9QZ

The Lake District National Park Authority
Murley Moss
Oxenholme Road
Kendal, Cumbria LA9 7RL

8   THE GEOLOGY OF THE LAKE DISTRICT

Nothing seems more permanent than mountains. But the shapes of the Lake District mountains tell of cataclysmal earth movements and violent upheavals. But all in the millions of years past? The enormity of geological time is extremely difficult to comprehend. The human life span is a cursory second of time in the infinite. But in the great timescale the mountains still move. The rocks are eroded by weather and are drawn down by gravity to the valleys. During rapid temperature changes you can see it happening on Wastwater Screes. On the other hand it is possible that the great granite mass which underlies much of the Lake District could be very gradually pushing upwards. The scenery is not static. It is dynamic.

The history of the Lake District over the last 530 million years can be seen in the landscape at the present time. The interpretation of some details has often caused some controversy, but there is general agreement on the major events.

The oldest rocks are the Skiddaw Slates. These were laid down in a shallow sea and later subjected to great pressure. Their age is usually put into the Ordovician period; some 530 million years ago. Most of this rock series now resembles shale rather than slate. It is minutely jointed and with the action of weather and frost has broken down into small flakes.

After the deposition of the Skiddaw Slates came several millions of years of volcanic action. Lava burst out from below the surface and flowed over the landscape. Explosions threw out hot 'bombs' of rock. Ash settled to huge depths. All this mass of varied material settled to a depth of up to two miles (three km) and formed what are known as the Borrowdale Volcanic series of rocks.

After that the whole area was covered by a shallow sea, and erosion material, at first calcareous, then huge amounts of grit and mud settled in layers to a depth of two and a half miles (four km). This was in the Silurian period between 440 and 410 million years ago.

It can be imagined that the then lakeless Lake District consisted of three thick layers of material each on top of the other. During the Devonian period the earth's crust was subject to much movement. The area was thrust upwards into a dome. Each of the rock types reacted differently according to the position of the centre of the thrust. Once the upper layers were fractured, for instance, the more malleable Skiddaw Slate beneath was pushed through to a great height, then hot sandstorms and heavy rains wore down the upper layers. Much of

Skiddaw Slates' topmost part, and a substantial area of the Silurian rocks were swept away. In the central parts the much harder Borrowdale Volcanics were left exposed. Therefore, the Skiddaw Slates were left uppermost in the north, the Volcanics in the centre, and the Silurian to the south.

Form 345 to 280 million years ago there followed the Carboniferous period. The area was again covered by a sea rich in life. The central part of the district probably remained as an island. The deposits in this sea formed the carboniferous limestone. Subsequently much of this was swept away leaving a rim around the Lake District. The Permo Trias period followed; the area became hot and arid. The desert sands of this time were later solidified into the New Red Sandstone, which again was mainly swept away from the central dome.

The tertiary period, 65 million years ago brought new upheavals to the planet. The 'Alpine' movement produced the Alps, the Himalayas and the Andes. Again the Lake District's dome was raised high. Fracture lines appeared, in general radiating from the centre, but varying in direction according to the reaction of the material. These formed the basis of the valley patterns we know today.

The next great catastrophe was nearer our own time. About one-and-a-half million years ago the climate changed dramatically and the whole of the northern hemisphere was covered in ice. The subsequent movement and melting of the ice hollowed out the valleys and lake beds, and swept away vegetation. The heavy rainstorms later moved any remaining loose material. Thus the dales were sculpted and the lakes were formed.

The visible history

What is seen now still reads historically from north to south. The mountains and hills of Skiddaw Slates which lie in a curving band, from the north to the west, are covered by carboniferous and sandstones nearer the coast, and reappear to the south-west at Black Combe. Because much of this material is shaley, craggy outcrops seldom occur. The fells have angular outlines. Typically of course there is Skiddaw itself (3054ft/930.8m) with its neighbour Saddleback (2847ft/867.7m). The fells to the west of Derwentwater, Causey Pike and Grisedale Pike, are of the same material, and the rock is also very evident in the fells on the east side of Buttermere, to the north and west around Crummock Water and Loweswater as well as the northern end of Ennerdale Water. There is good soil depth on these rock forms which allows trees and heather to grow naturally.

In the central Lake District roughly north-east to south-west are the high craggy fells of the Borrowdale Volcanics. The soaring walls of the Scafells, Great Gable, the Borrowdale fells, as well as Coniston Old Man in the south-west through the Langdales and Bowfell; and eastwards through Helvellyn to High Street; these are all examples of Borrowdale Volcanics. They excite the interest of rock-climbers and mountaineers. As the iron-hard rock does not break down easily the minerals are 'locked in' and the shallow acidic soils do not support a rich vegetation. The alpine plants are found mainly where springs leach the minerals to the surface. The deeper soils are often covered in bracken, beautifully coloured in autumn, but useless to the hill farmers' sheep. From the hard 'tuff' in this series of rocks Neolithic settlers hammered out stone axes and exported them to many parts of Britain. From another type of rock, formed from fine volcanic sediments in water, come the famous green-slate, still quarried and much in demand for its wearing and decorative qualities. It is used for the facings of prestigious buildings.

The Silurian rock types are visible in the south of the Lake District. These soft slates and mudstones produce an acid soil in which trees and forests find root and regenerate quite readily. The typical scenery, much in evidence around Windermere, consists of rounded hills, often with a good deal of tree cover. The Forestry Commission's largest forest, at Grizedale is also in this area.

The limestones and the sandstones are round the fringe of the district. There are several exposures of granite. Granites are Plutons, formed from Volcanic material cooling slowly beneath the earth's crust. The Lake District granites were probably formed during the Devonian earth movements when cavities and fractures in the rocks became filled with the super-heated magma thrust up from the depths of the earth. The granites were uncovered by later erosion and notably these can be seen at Shap in the north-east, or on the north end of the Helvellyn range near Threlkeld. There are also exposures of granite types in Eskdale, Wasdale, and Ennerdale to the west. These Plutonic 'bubbles' are surrounded by rocks much changed by the tremendous heat; metamorphic. The zone between is known as the metamorphic aureole. The cracks in the metamorphic rocks were sometimes filled with molten minerals and here are found the metals notable in the Lake District, iron, copper and lead. The metals were mined from Roman times until early this century. The more productive mines were in the Newlands Valley and the western side of Derwentwater, and at Greenside, above Glenridding on the side of Helvellyn.

The last effect of the landscape was man-made. Before there was substantial human settlement the whole area was covered in forest. This has been removed over a period of four thousand years. Much of it was destroyed from early Elizabethan times up to the last century to provide charcoal for the hungry iron furnaces. The increase in sheep grazing has meant that regeneration has been impossible. Much of the woodland and forest we now see was planted within the last century and a half. The lack of tree cover in places has accelerated erosion and impoverished the soil.

Walk 1
CIRCUIT OF ENNERDALE WATER
7½ miles (12km) Fairly strenuous; some rough ground

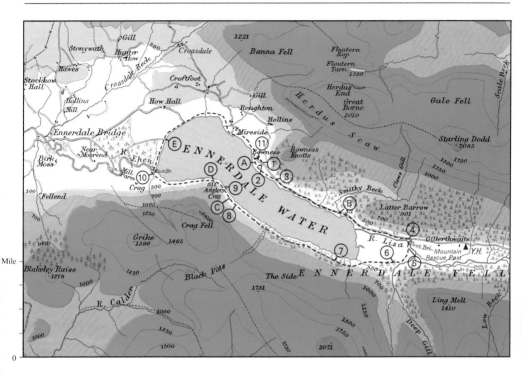

The views over Ennerdale Water suggest peace and awesome tranquility. Yet the dale has been the subject of heated controversy. There was very little when the lake was turned into a reservoir for this had minimal effect; but it was different when the Forestry Commission acquired most of the valley in the 1920s, displacing 2000 sheep and replacing them by many thousands of dark conifers, restricting free access to the area previously enjoyed by walkers. Despite protest the Forestry Commission won. More recently, in the 1980s, the Water Authority wished to raise the dam and flood a wide area. They were defeated by the combined weight of the Conservationists and the National Park Special Planning Board. If the Water Authority had won, this walk would have been impossible. Ennerdale is a deep crystal-clear lake. Around its head is the rock known as Ennerdale granophyre, a very hard mainly pink granite which breaks down into irregular blocks making walking, away from the made-up tracks, very uneven and thus more tiring than hazardous. The one apparent hazard on the walk is the steep side of Angling Crag. The path here is narrow but quite negotiable. This walk is adventurous and the memorable view across the lake, particularly upwards to the heights of Pillar and Steeple, are enough to set the senses tingling.

Strong, well-cleated footwear is essential. If the walk is to be savoured it is best to take a picnic lunch and spend most of the day on the walk. The walk begins at the car park provided by the Forestry Commission at Bowness Knott. To reach this, take the minor road from Croasdale north-east of Ennerdale Bridge.

12

Walk 1
Circuit of Ennerdale Water
continued

1 *Leave the car park and walk up the hill opposite, to the viewpoint.*

A Viewpoint here gives a superb view over the lake. Across the lake is Anglers' Crag. Contrast the view up the lake from here to the high fells, with the milder country down the lake. The high craggy land belongs to the Borrowdale Volcanic series of rocks. Around the upper part of the lake and behind us is the hard Ennerdale Granophyre, but down the lake are the soft shales of the Skiddaw Slates. When the moving ice of the Ice Age carved out the valley it was squeezed by the hard rocks, and then fanned out over the softer shale to give the lake its distinct shape.

2 *Walk down to the lakeshore. Continue left on the lakeshore path.*

3 *Join forest road and continue on.*

B 'Smithy Beck' suggests a rural industry now gone. In fact before the valley was depopulated, for the sake of timber and water supplies, the valley had been settled extensively since Viking incursions in the 10th century.

4 *Just beyond the Forestry Commission's causeway across the river, a path right leads down to a footbridge. Cross this.*

5 *After the bridge go left, then right to cross the field footpath.*

6 *Do not go through a gate into the plantation but go right with the wall, over stiles.*

7 *Follow the lakeside path.*

8 *Go through the wall gap.*

C Viewpoint for lake head with Red Pike and High Stile to north.

9 *To skirt Anglers' Crag the path rises, then undulates, awkwardly in places, before descending to the lakeshore.*

D The geological change should be seen on the shoreline here.

10 *Cross bridge and proceed along the causeway to pick up the lakeshore path.*

E Another splendid viewpoint which was once the site of the famous *Anglers Hotel* but now regretfully demolished under threat of eventual immersion.

11 *Follow the track leaving the lakeshore and return to the starting point.*

Walk 2
ROUND LOWESWATER
4 miles (6.4 km) Easy

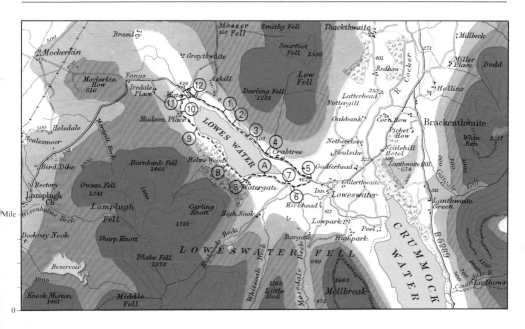

Loweswater is in the softer landscape of the Skiddaw Slate. The material is more properly described as a shale which breaks down to give a reasonable depth of soil. This means that much of the area not heavily grazed by stock is woodland. Lovely Loweswater, bordered by trees, is in the care of The National Trust. The lake is little more than a mile (1.6km) long and its circuit is an easy and pleasing stroll. Like most of the lakes, Loweswater probably takes its name from an ancient Norse owner; in this case Laghi; 'Laghi's Water'. The lake is unique in the Lake District in that its outflow flows in; that is the flow goes inwards (eastwards) towards the District's centre. It flows, in fact, into Crummock Water before

that lake flows outwards to the north as the River Cocker.

1 Start the walk from a terraced lay-by to the north-east of the lake, between the road and the lake. Walk by the lake on the road.
2 Walk down and along the lake shore when possible.
3 If the water level is high you might have to walk on the road for a short distance.
4 Go left, back to the road, at a fence. Walk along the road.
5 Turn right and go down a tarmacadam lane.
6 After the curves in the road, watch for a gate on the right, for Watergate.
7 Go through the gate and along the track.

A Viewpoint over the field to the lake.
8 At Watergate, go through the gates and along the lakeside path.
B Tree spotters can note the wide variety of hardwoods grown here. As this is National Trust land there is freedom to wander and identify species or to linger on the shore.
9 Continue on the path alongside the wall and away from the lake.
10 Hudson Place. Turn right and go down a 'hollow lane'.
11 There is a choice of paths here. Go straight on, or turn right to cut the corner through a gate, over a slate bridge, then over a wooden bridge to the gate at the roadside.
12 Join the road and turn right to the starting point.

14

Walk 3
WALLA CRAG
6½ miles (10.5 km) 1000 ft (304.8 m) Strenuous

No other part of Britain can offer so many superb views in so small a area. Walla Crag is one of the more spectacular with views over the whole of Derwentwater to Bassenthwaite Lake, up into the jaws of Borrowdale, and to most of the major mountains. The walk is fairly strenuous but the reasonably fit can do it with no trouble; some people will take longer than others. There is plenty to see if the weather is clear; if visibility is poor the walk should not be attempted. It is advisable to carry some food with you. Strong footwear with good ground grip is necessary. The walk starts along Derwentwater shore.

1 *The walk starts in Keswick. Walk down to the boat landings.*

2 *Continues on the pathway to its end.*

A Friars Crag - a much photographed view up the lake and into the jaws of Borrowdale. Here, it is said, friars would wait to obtain a blessing from St Herbert. The saint lived in his hermitage on St Herbert's island in the 7th century.

3 *Continue on the path round the bay and beyond The Ings.*

4 *Walk down to the lakeshore again by Stable Hills, and round Calf Close Bay.*

5 *Follow the path to the road, through a gap, and across the road into Great*

Wood opposite. Continue until the main car parking area is reached. Join another path here.

6 *There is a stile and sign to 'Ashness'. Follow this recently made path along the hillside.*

B All praise to The National Trust for this path which reveals such splendid views over the lake.

7 *The path joins a minor road to Ashness. Turn left up it.*

8 *Near an old gateway (before reaching stone-arched Ashness Bridge) a path starts on the left. Follow this up the fell.*

C Good view over Derwentwater to Bassenthwaite.

9 *Path junction. Continue straight on.*

D The summit. Derwentwater is visible in all its splendour at a dizzy depth below. Behind is Causey Pike and to the right and beyond is Grisedale Pike. Look left up Borrowdale to see Scafell Pike, Scafell, and Great Gable. The Skiddaw range and Saddleback are towards the right and with your back to the cairn the Helvellyn range is in full view to the south-east.

10 *Walk on from the cairn on a path downwards following a fence. Follow it on to a bridge.*

11 *Cross bridge and on to a metalled road. Follow it on.*

12 *Go left over the footbridge.*

13 *Continue right on pathway.*

14 *Path junction. Continue straight on.*

15 *Join roadway.*

16 *At this point a detour left is recommended to take in yet another viewpoint from Castlehead, a remarkable boss of rock overlooking the lake.*

17 *Return to roadway and back to starting point.*

Walk 4
SOUTHER FELL
5 miles (8km) Moderate; wet areas; circuit

1 *Start at the Inn and bridge. Walk on until a lane is reached; a short distance on the left. Walk past the farm and on up an old mine track.*

2 *At the junction go left. The left-hand route is less clear on the ground.*

3 *Wet areas can be avoided with care by going upwards above them or down to the stony ground.*

A This is a pleasant secluded dale with a passive rather than dramatic aspect.

4 *Wet areas can be avoided with care.*

5 *Go down an angled path to a bridge and cross to a path going left on the far side of the river.*

B Good view down the valley and upwards to the northern end of Saddleback proper; the narrow ridge is known as 'Sharp Edge'.

C This is the summit of the path from which there is a view south to Helvellyn. If it is a clear day the central fells may be seen, with Scafell Pike, the highest point in England (3210ft/978m) to the south-west.

6 *Descend, avoiding the wet areas as far as possible, to the gate and on to a lane. Go left and follow the lane right through. If the gates are closed, open and then close them after you. The lane goes on to the Inn.*

D The rock here is *Skiddaw Slate*; really a sort of shale. Where water reaches the surface it leaches out minerals which provide a rich environment for a great variety of wild flowers to grow.

E The Inn was once a mill. The location could hardly have been better.

Souther is pronounced 'Sowter'. It is a spur off the mountain of Saddleback (otherwise Celtic 'Blencathra') and is unusual as it is almost completely surrounded by river; the Glenderamackin. Glenderamackin is another Celtic name; the area has Celtic connections, such as the nearby Carrock Fell where there are remains of a Celtic hill fort. It is said that a force of warriors haunts Souther Fell on Midsummer's Eve, but there has been no record of a sighting since the 18th century. At that time on several Midsummer Eves the column was led by mounted officers. With so much detail in the tales they may well be true!

The walk starts at the village of Mungrisdale. 'Grisdale', 'Grizedale' or 'Grisedale' abounds as a place name in the Lake District and this is Norse for 'dale of pigs'. Here the Celtic prefix 'Mung' ('Mungho' in another name) means 'dearest one'. It refers to the 7th century Celtic missionary St Kentigern to whom Mungrisdale's church is dedicated.

There is still a brooding Celtic mystery about the fell and the quiet circuit is an antidote to the noisy reality of the 20th century. Mungrisdale is reached from the A66 at a junction seven miles (11.3km) from Keswick and eight (12.9km) from Penrith.

Walk 5
GREENSIDE
3½ miles (5.6 km) Easy

Once Greenside, in an eastern valley of Helvellyn above the village of Glenridding, had one of the most profitable lead mines in the north of England. It was in production from the late 18th century to the middle of this one. It was reckoned that by 1876 it had produced some 40 000 tons (40 642 tonnes) of smelted lead, and 600 000 oz (24 000g) of silver. In 1891 electrical winding gear was introduced. It was the first metal mine in the country to use it. The workings were extremely intensive and went deep into Helvellyn. An electrical locomotive (another first) was also used for drawing material from the productive shafts a mile (1.6km) into the mountain. Originally this work was done by seven horses. Compressed air, for driving the drills, was provided by electricity. By modern standards the generating plant and installations were crude and dangerous, but they were worked with little mishap. Ore was smelted

on the site and the furnace flue was carried one and a half miles (2.4km) up the mountain so that lead vapour could condense on the flue sides to be collected for return to the furnace. Water power was provided from the falls of Red Tarn and Kepple Cove Tarn above, the latter was dammed. This dam burst in a great storm in 1927 and a wall of water smashed through the workings and the village causing great damage, but miraculously no loss of life. The remaining sign of this disaster is the promontory on Ullswater formed from the debris and on which the steamer pier now stands.

Hardly anything remains of the works buildings and all is silent now. The mine was sealed in 1962 after the Atomic Energy Authority conducted seismic tests with conventional explosives deep in the workings. The old 'tailing dams' consisting of vast quantities of waste material were partly covered by the mining company, with grass and

trees and further work is being done by the National Park Special Planning Board who now own the site. The walk uses the old mine track and a pleasant airy route following an old aqueduct.

1 *The walk starts at the Glenridding car park. Turn left and go up the road through the village estate.*

2 *Turn right at end of village, then left again on rough roadway past a line of terraced cottages and on up the valley via the track.*

A Little building on the right was the gunpowder store which was always situated well away from the main workings. Few other buildings remain; now two are being used as hostels. Note the stabilisation work on the surface of the tailing dams.

3 *Continue straight on up a track parallel to the beck which pounds dizzily below.*

4 *Cross footbridge to a path on other side of the beck and turn left on it.*

5 *Continue on the clear line of an old aqueduct which now makes a pleasant pathway.*

B Pleasant view left. The illusion is given that the walk on this aqueduct is down hill or level. In fact this is not so. Water was collected and taken back to the workings behind.

6 *Leave the aqueduct line and descend to the signed footpath below. Follow this path through.*

7 *The path joins the track, descend on it.*

8 *Do not cross the bridge, but turn on the riverside path back to village.*

Walk 6
ESKSIDE RAMBLE AND DALEGARTH WATERFALLS
4 miles (6.4km) Moderate; some rough sections.

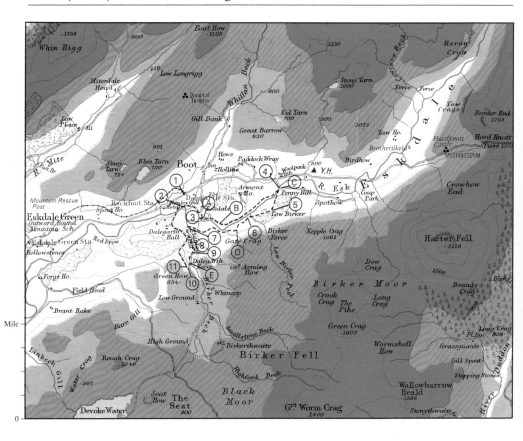

Eskdale lacks only a lake; but it has everything else. It is a long dale with its head under the highest land in England and its foot in the sea, and it has an incredible variety of landscape types. It would take a lifetime to explore it thoroughly. It has a history too. Down this dale came the stone axes roughed out by Neolithic craftsmen. They were then carried to the coastal sandstone for polishing and sharpening. The Romans improved the Anglo Saxon road and built a fort on one of the dale's spectacular vantage points, at Hardknott, and another to guard their port at the dale's foot at Ravenglass. Then followed the Viking settlements. After the Norman conquest the monks of Furness Abbey claimed much of the valley, managing the deer herds and probably opening the first iron mines here which produced high quality ore until the 19th century. The middle and lower reaches of the dale are walled by crags of granite, much of it coloured pink by the iron content. In one great wooded ravine in its southern side there flows a beautiful waterfall, known as both Dalegarth Falls and Stanley Ghyll Force. This walk follows the river side, past the dale's little church, and finishes by climbing up alongside the waterfall to an airy viewpoint on top of a precipice.

18

Walk 6
Eskside Ramble and Dalegarth Waterfalls
continued

1 *There are two possible starting points. One is at Dalegarth Station, the terminus of the narrow-gauge railway ('The Ratty') for anyone arriving by train from Ravenglass, or using the station car park. In which case it is necessary to walk a short distance back down the valley to the left turning by the little war memorial. The walk then begins at a turning left between the walls a little way along this road. Alternatively, the walk can be started from the car park down the Dalegarth road, walking back to cross the bridge. The path starts at the first turning on the right.*
2 *The path leads to St Catherine's Church.*

A A Chapel was established in Eskdale as long ago as the 12th century. In the 15th century the chapel was promoted to a parish church. This upgrading followed a successful petition to the Pope which complained about the hardships experienced in travelling to St Bees for burials and baptisms. The church was rebuilt in 1881. In the church-yard there are two interesting gravestones to two notable huntsmen, Tommy Dobson and Willy Porter.

3 *On leaving the church, follow the path left by the river bank.*

B There are some beautiful clear pools in the river bed. Look for the remains of a mine bridge for transport of the ore via the railway.

4 *Cross the stone bridge.*

C Attractive arch bridge of local stone.

5 *Just above Low Birker farm, turn right on to a clear track.*
6 *The track continues parallel with the river.*

D Signs of mining activity around include very red earth, and waste tips.

7 *Cross the bridge, walk up the bank and go left to follow the gill side to join clear path.*
8 *Cross two bridges.*
9 *Viewpoint bridge. The true path turns here, but the fit and agile might scramble a little further for more views of falls, but they must return to this point. Double back and go upwards from here turning left at a T-junction, over a little beck and up to a viewpoint.*

E Those with no head for heights will have to be content with standing back. *Children should be closely controlled.* The crag falls sheer into the gill at this point, but there is a grand view northwards over the Eskdale valley, which is framed by trees.

10 *Leave this viewpoint and follow the path to a stile over the wall, which joins a good track.*
11 *Turn right and follow the track past Dalegarth Hall to your starting point.*

Walk 7
LOWER DUDDON AND FRITH HALL
5 miles (8km) Moderate

1730 seventeen marriages were recorded. In 1736 a guest met a mysterious end. He was possibly murdered. His ghost is said to haunt the place.

1 *The walk starts south of Ulpha Bridge. A parking space can usually be found by the roadside. Walk to the bridge.*

2 *Cross the bridge and turn left along the road.*

3 *Just after the second bridge on this road note what was once a mill on the right. Continue on.*

A Much use was made of the running water in these valleys. Here at one time timber from the surrounding coppice woods, was turned to provide bobbins for the Lancashire textile industry.

4 *After the road levels out look for a small bridle gate to the left. Go through this and follow the wall.*

5 *Cross the stile in the wall. Join the track and turn right, go over bridge and on.*

B Frith Hall ruin. Good views from a very 'atmospheric' prospect.

6 *Continue down the old track which becomes pleasant walking. The track descends to the road.*

7 *Turn left and follow the road down.*

8 *Go left down the track (signed as Mill Bridge and Mill How) towards the houses, over a bridge.*

9 *Go over a second bridge, by the farmyard and down a track through trees, which follows on by the woodland and plantations. Wet areas can be avoided with care.*

10 *The track curves left.*

11 *Join the road and go right to the starting point.*

The River Duddon is a delight throughout its route. Two roads, either side of the Duddon's lower reaches join at Ulpha (Scandinavian 'ulf-hauga' meaning 'wolf hill'). On whichever road you travel your eyes are drawn to a ruined 'castle' on the hill between. This is Frith Hall, high on the ancient roadway. It is not a castle, but a former hunting lodge for the Ulpha deer park owned by the Huddleston family. At the end of the 16th century it became an Inn. In the 18th century the Inn got itself a reputation. It became a sort of 'Gretna Green'; in

Walk 8
THE BEACON AND BEACON TARN
3¾ miles (6km) 700ft (213.3m) Moderate; some wet sections

There are beacon points all over Britain and historically they were part of a fairly rapid nation-wide communications system. The sites were chosen so as to be visible from a large area and it should therefore follow that they offer the best viewpoints. The beacon on Blawith Fell overlooking the southern end of Coniston Water is a good example, even though it is of modest height at 835 feet (254.5m). A walk to it would be reward enough, but this route goes by Beacon Tarn, a lovely piece of water which sits below the fell, and this high area is attractive heather moor. Blawith Fell is part of a common in the care of the National Park, so you are free to wander or linger anywhere, but this route is recommended one.

1 *Park at a car parking area on Blawith Common. This is an open area south of Brown Howe on the Torver - Ulverston road, and a mile (1.6km) north of Water Yeat. Walk down the roadside with care, south towards Ulverston.*

2 *After a bend there is an open area with a stream on the right. From here* a path can be seen going up the hillside through the bracken. Follow this. It meanders as it climbs and goes between knolls.

3 *The path descends to a footbridge which can be seen below.*

4 *Cross the footbridge and pick up the path following the beck. Follow it right round the tarn on its western side.*

A Enjoy the quiet tarn. The word 'tarn' has a Norse origin from their word 'tjorn'. Height has only a little to do with why some stretches of water are called tarns and other lakes. Brother's Water (a lake) for instance, is roughly the same height as this tarn. The practised eye can usually tell the difference; there is less luxurious vegetation around a tarn. The Freshwater Biological Association explains the difference between a lake and a tarn in this way. A lake's characteristic emergent plant is the common reed, while in a tarn it is the bottle sedge. In the boggy areas around a tarn two small insectiverous plants can be found. They are the sundew with its round red sticky 'dewy' leaves by which it traps insects and the butterwort, which has broad smooth

sticky leaves lying flat and looks like a small green starfish. The sundew can easily be missed as it merges so well with the moss.

5 *Go right round the top of the tarn to pick up a footpath going up into the fell, Follow this through and along the ridge.*

6 *Just before the path begins a descent take a detour left to Beacon summit.*

B The summit view is mainly eastwards and southwards. Notably one can see the whole length of Coniston Water, surely the best view of the lake from any point. The value as a beacon point can be seen. To the south-west is the hump of Black Combe, the site of another beacon which could take signals and pass them on from as far away as Merseyside and the Isle of Man. Far off to the east the Pennines where there are several beacon points can be seen. One can see over to Morecambe Bay. To the north-east there is Helvellyn on the left and the High Street range on the right. To the north-west the view is dominated by the Coniston Old Man range. Dow Crag, the popular rock-climbing cliff is the high point on the left with the lesser peaks of Buck Pike and Brown Pike to the left again. The central fell is the Old Man and Wetherlam is the body of the fell to the right and behind. Natural little rock gardens on the outcrops, are charming features of this area.

7 *Rejoin the path and start the descent. Several paths join together.*

8 *Join metalled lane and go right.*

9 *Join road and go right to starting point.*

Walk 9
BIRKS BRIDGE AND SEATHWAITE, DUNNERDALE
6 miles (9.6km) Moderate

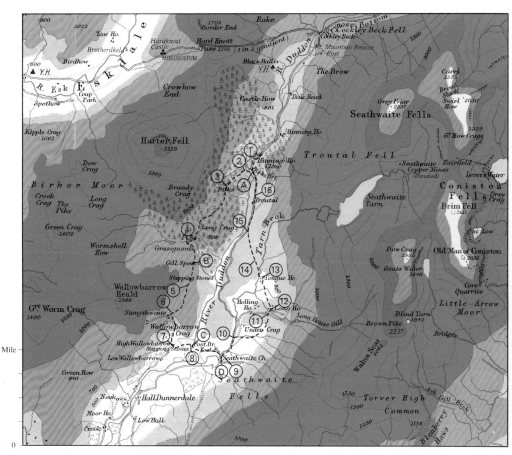

Of all the Lake District rivers the Duddon is surely the most sublime. Wordsworth thought so and wrote a poem entitled *The River Duddon,* from which this stanza is taken.

'All hail, ye mountains: hail,
    thou morning light!
Better to breathe at large on this
    clear height
Than toil in the needless
    sleep from dream to dream:

Pure flow the verse, pure,
    vigorous, free and bright,
For Duddon, long-loved
    Duddon, is my theme!'

The Duddon rises on the fells above Wrynose and can be a gentle flow or a frenzied torrent. The valley it flows through is tree clad, green and serene. This walk starts above the famous Birks Bridge.

1 *Park in the Forestry Commission* car park near the valley head, and walk back down the road.

A The bridge here is a thing of beauty itself, but do look into the green water and see how the torrent and spinning stones have sculpted the hard bed rock.

2 *Cross the bridge and take the path going right then turn sharp left to the Birks.*

Walk 9
Birks Bridge and Seathwaite, Dunnerdale
continued

3 *Keep left on the forest tracks and cross the footbridge to Grassguards.*

4 *Go through the yard and down the track between the walls.*

B Look at the drystone walls on either side of the track; a beautiful example of the waller's art.

5 *Path to an open fell.*

6 *Just before Stoneythwaite farm go left to follow the wall and which falls steeply to High Wallowbarrow.*

7 *Go towards the farm, then turn left alongside the barn and go through the stile to pick up the path on the grassy terrace left.*

C Some pretty rock pools here under the fine arched bridge.

8 *Go over the bridge, walk up the path by the wall and over a slate bridge, then on to cross an old mill race by another. Continue on the path and cross two more bridges to the roadside and Seathwaite Church.*

D No visit to Seathwaite is complete without learning about 'Wonderful Walker' who lived here as curate of the little church for 66 years and died in 1802 at the age of 92. His stipend was £50 *per annum*, and yet, despite giving to the poor, he still had £200 left in his will. He worked hard as an itinerant farm worker, taught the children and healed the sick. There is a brass plate to his memory on the wall. The stone where he sat to shear sheep is in the yard not far from his wife's grave. She lived until she was 81.

9 *Go up the road.*

10 *Take the turning right for Turner Hall. On this road continue on but ignore the right turn. On reaching the T-junction turn left and go directly on a track ignoring the right turn. Keep left of the buildings.*

11 *Join the road and go left and immediately turn sharp right and towards Long House.*

12 *Cross the bridge and turn sharp left on the path between the walls. Go through the stile and over the bridge to Tongue House farmyard.*

13 *Go forward to the road, turn left for a short distance, then cross the footbridge on the right. Follow the wall by the catwalk. Walk in front of the house by the wood and then cross over the stile. Climb up through the woods.*

14 *Follow the incline right over the hillside on green path. The path is less distinct, but walk on towards Harter Fell ahead. Cross over the stile and descend to the road.*

15 *Go right on the road.*

16 *Pick up riverside path to Birks Bridge, then follow the road to the car park.*

Walk 10
TILBERTHWAITE AND LITTLE LANGDALE
4 miles (6.4km) 1000ft (304.8km) Moderate; some very steep, rough, wet sections

There is some steep ground on this route so sandals, wellington boots or smooth-soled shoes are out. Remember that steep grass can be as treacherous as rock. Old mine shafts are another hazard for those whose curiosity may lure them from the path; though the more dangerous ones are fenced. Children and dogs should be kept carefully controlled. Lone walkers should take the precaution of leaving route details with someone at 'base'. Although this

walk has these disadvantages the rewards are great. It starts by the waterfall, which is very spectacular after rain and goes via ancient copper mines. After making the ascent to the walk's highest point any breath left could be taken away by the awesome, symphonic (Wagnerian?) view over Langdale.

1 *Park in the old quarry parking area at the foot of Tilberthwaite Gill, which is reached by a minor road off the Coniston to Ambleside road. As-*

cend by the path rising on the left-hand side of the gill, following the gill's course at the higher level.

2 *Bear right and descend to cross the gill by the footbridge. Then follow rough scrambly path and stone steps to the bridge.*

A Viewpoint. The fall seen here is only 20 feet (6m) but the volume of water is often very great. The upper falls cannot be reached. Earlier this century more bridges and catwalks

24

were in position above this viewpoint bridge, but they have been swept away by massive floods which have torn down the unstable walls of the ravine.

3 *Go back from the viewpoint bridge some 16 yards (14.6m) then climb up the narrow rough path which rises steeply to the left.*

4 *Follow this path upwards, over a stile, to join the old miners' track. Go left up it.*

5 *At top of the gill ravine, go right on the old miners' track.*

B Everywhere there are signs of copper mine workings; spoil heaps and ruins. The veins of ore going east and west here have been exploited since ancient times. This side of the Coniston Old Man range is riddled with holes like a maggoty cheese. There is some evidence that copper was mined here in Roman times, though inevitably many of the signs of old workings have been destroyed by more recent activity. The last major efforts in this area, including the driving of a 500 fathom level (914m), and the sinking of a 65 fathom shaft (118.87m), occurred in 1850, but extraction proved too costly and the main production became concentrated in the Coniston Copper Mines to the south-west, and at Greenburn to the north.

6 *At this point, near the old mine workings and stonework where the track goes sharply left for a steep (and eroded) ascent to Wetherlam,* **go right,** *upwards on a less distinct path past old mine workings and stonework. Beware of the collapsed and dangerous shaft.*

7 *At the top of this 'saddle' look directly below to see a fairly indistinct path to the right of a fence and a bog. Take care on this steep descent.*

C There are many fine views of Langdale Pikes but surely none to cap this! Sit here and look. In the foreground there is a tumble of crags and between Blake Rigg and Lingmoor, Blea Tarn can be seen. This is the type of landscape which burst like a bomb on the early tourists' eyes in their discovery of the Lake District in the 18th century. 'Langdale Pikes hold their ragged heads in shapeless horror' wrote Budworth in a book at that time. 'Horror' was a popular word for the writers of the day when describing the district. Then, it was used to mean excitement rather than terror. Perhaps television and easy travel today has made us rather more blasé about scenery. But this view cannot fail to stir. It is surely one of the best mountain prospects in Britain.

8 *Go over the stile and walk on the right. Follow wall down to a high step stile.*

9 *Go over this, then go left of beck and follow wall, with care, by the steep fragmentary path interspersed with grass tussocks and wet ground.*

10 *Join the miners' track and go right.*

D Enjoy further marvellous views over to Langdale Pikes. Here the foreground is a rocky chaos, a turmoil of craggy shapes, adding more drama. Forward is Little Langdale Tarn. The road over Wrynose begins below in Little Langdale. The modern road follows the old Roman road (the *Xth iter*) over the pass, linking the fort at Ambleside with the fort at Hardknott and on to Ravenglass. Its route until it reaches the farm of Fell Foot below is not traceable, but from there onwards it is to the north, that is the far side, of the present road.

11 *Track junction. Go upwards to the right and follow the quarry track straight onwards (detours lead to quarries).*

E Extensive quarrying to the right. The quarrying boom followed the copper mining. To win the copper the mining engineers had to break through the very hard volcanic rock. When the copper prices fell because of cheap imports, and the steel shipbuilding lessened the demand for copper plates which sheathed the hulls of wooden vessels, the sales potential of the fine hard slate was realised. The mine waste heaps became buried under quarry waste as the boom continued. Sometimes the slate was actually mined, when the levels of higher class material were followed into the mountain side. A detour to look at the slate might be of interest. The colour varies in each locality. The material was formed from volcanic dust laid down under water and the ripple marks can sometimes be seen. The slate is hard and takes a good polish. In the boom in the 19th century records show that a quarryman was paid a guinea (£1.05) for working a six day week.

12 *The track finishes at a gate (close it afterwards) and a surfaced lane is reached. Go right, by the farm, to the starting point.*

Walk 11
TARN HOWS FROM HAWKSHEAD
6 miles (9.7km) 500ft (152.4m) Moderate

Tarn Hows is visited by thousands of people each year. It is the best known beauty spot in the Lake District and indeed one of the best known in Britain. Some people prefer to steer clear of the popular, but Tarn Hows cannot be ignored. It is a jewel of a tarn with little promontories and islands all set among a happy mixture of trees, hardwoods and conifers, with the spectacular backdrop of Langdale Fells. It is a perfectly balanced scene, best viewed in early spring in its many shades of green; or in the autumn's blaze. It can be marred only perhaps on hot days when too many people congregate around the water's edge and so break up the picture's foreground. In high summer, for this reason, it is best enjoyed in the early morning or late evening. This walk goes all the way from Hawkshead, returning by what is known as 'the mountain road'.

1 The start is at Hawkshead church. Walk through the churchyard and on to path beyond.

2 Take the path bearing right to join a minor road.

3 Cross the minor road and take the path, signposted, across the fields.

4 Join the road, turn left up it.

5 Turn right at the first junction.

6 Cross the road and go up the one signposted Tarn Hows.

7 Look for a stile over the wall on the left. Cross it and go on with the wall for a short distance, then over another stile and continue.

8 Walk across to the wall corner, take the stile which goes over into wood (not the one straight on).

A A most pleasant wood to begin as it has a mixture of trees. Further on the trees are mainly larch. All this area is in the care of The National Trust.

9 Walk on through the wood to a path junction close to a minor road.

10 Do **not** join road but go left before it to follow the wall on a path which runs parallel to the road.

11 Join the road at the hill top and walk on the left overlooking the tarn.

B There are many viewpoints here. Take your choice!

12 Descend to the dam wall and follow the main path going from it.

13 Watch for a turn left to leave the tarn. It is approached after rising and descending on a rocky portion of path, and just as the tarn is seen close ahead. Cross the stile and go forward on a pleasant walk through open woodland.

14 Join a rough, unmetalled road. Go up to the right.

C Viewpoint near crest of hill. Left for unusual view of Langdale Pikes. On the extreme left but closer is Wetherlam.

D View of Ambleside left over the gate. Esthwaite Water ahead.

15 Join the road and go down the minor road almost immediately opposite.

16 After passing buildings and crossing a little bridge go right (signed) across a field. The path is obscure here. Aim for a point to the right of the wooded knoll ahead.

17 Pinch stile ('fatman's agony') in the wall. Go through this and on with wall on the left, go on the same line.

18 Go through the gate, bear right through another gate, and on over a cattle bridge right of the buildings to a gate opposite a telephone box and on to the road.

19 Turn left and retrace to Hawkshead.

Walk 12
EASEDALE TARN
5 miles (8km) 620ft (188.9m) Moderate; wet underfoot

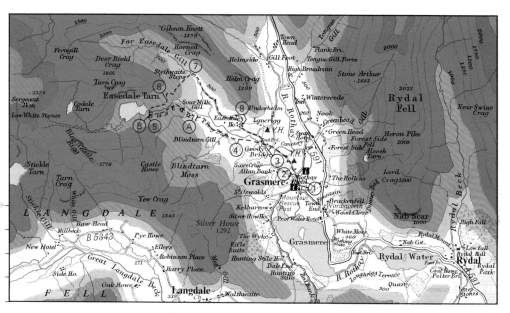

When the Wordsworths lived at Grasmere in the early 19th century they called Easedale 'the black quarter' for that is where the bad weather comes from before it hits the village. Dorothy Wordworth's journal makes several references to their many walks up Easedale, sometimes in search of mosses, but often to enjoy the sight of the waterfall they called 'Churn-milk force' now known as Sour Milk Gill. William, once when in sad mood as he approached the tarn was cheered by the appearance of a rainbow which inspired his small poem, *My Heart Leaps Up* from which these lines are taken.

'My heart leaps up when I behold
A rainbow in the sky'.

Once Dorothy turned back from the walk, frightened when con-fronted by a cow. Nothing much has changed since then. The falling white water is still a spectacle after heavy rain. The round tarn in its arena of high fells is still a pleasant sight. Perhaps the cows are more placid than they used to be!

This is a favourite short walk from Grasmere marred only by some wet ground which is avoid-able by a wide detour. After heavy rain the stepping-stones at the tarn outlet might be impassable, which would mean a return by the out-ward route. Strong footwear is essential.

1 *Start the walk in Grasmere village.*
2 *Take the minor road going north-west from the village centre, near the Heaton Cooper studio.*

3 *Turn left when the road reaches the riverside to cross bridges, and follow the good track on.*
4 *Go through the gate and on across the field to another gate and to start the climb.*
A Water cascade. An approach can be made with care.
B Tarn outlet. A good view over the tarn from the high bank.
5 *Cross the stepping stones, turn right and follow the path which eventually curves left.*
6 *Boggy ground. The worst can be avoided by a very wide sweep left to the higher ground and back.*
7 *Cross the bridge and follow the path down on the far bank. It changes to a track after a rough descent section.*
8 *Track joins tarmacadam road. Follow this down to join the minor road to starting point.*

Walk 13
TROUTBECK AND WANSFELL PIKE FROM AMBLESIDE
6 miles (9.7km) Strenuous

This walk has a feast of varied attractions. It offers some of the best viewpoints over the northern reaches of Windermere and to the central fells. It is a walk through a renowned and unspoilt 17th century village (with a chance to look inside one of the houses owned by the National Trust); a walk up to another viewpoint at an airy 1500ft (457.2m) with a very wide panoramic view and as a grand finale, particularly after heavy rain, a look at one of the best known waterfalls. All this cannot be achieved without encountering a few snags such as wet sections of path, a steady climb up a low fell and a steep descent. The walk should be done in clear

weather. Some people might find the thought of a climb rather daunting but anyone who is reasonably fit should be able to cope, especially if the walk is taken at a leisurely pace. A visit to Town End, the house owned by The National Trust and open to the public, is well worthwhile. Take a picnic lunch and make a day of it.

1 *Park in Ambleside and walk south towards Windermere from the town centre. Take the old Lake Road left from the main road.*
2 *Go left upwards on a narrow tarmac lane.*
3 *Keep right on the contour with views and enter the woodland.*

4 *Look for The National Trust sign on the right ('Jenkin Crag') and divert on the path to the viewpoint.*
A A viewpoint from a craggy spur with superb views over the lake to the central fells.
5 *After crossing the bridge turn upwards from the well-defined way through a field.*
6 *Join Robin Lane.*
7 *Look for the stone cairn up in the field on the left. Walk up to it.*
B Another spectacular viewpoint.
8 *Go down the lane on the right to join the road and go left.*
C Town End; the 17th century house open to the public. Go into the village. Note the 'bank barn'

28

opposite Town End. This barn design is a typical old Lake District one. Hay is taken in at the high floor level and fed to the cattle which enter at the 'ground floor' below. This type of barn is typical of those found in Scandinavia, thus giving further credence to the belief that there was extensive Viking settlement in ancient times in the Lake District. Walk on through the village and note the interesting architectural features. The buildings are all built from stone slate, quarried locally. The oldest are 17th century but there was further building during the more prosperous period of the 18th and 19th centuries. The large cylindrical chimneys are tradi-tional in the district. The village is really a succession of hamlets, each grouped round the communal wells, which are named after saints; St John, St James, St Margaret. Unusually, the church is hidden away outside and below the village. This was because it had to serve several settlements scattered all over the valley.

9 *After St Margaret's Well watch for the signed path going left from a barn end for Wansfell Pike, but divert first along the road if you wish to see an interesting old sign at the* Mortal Man. *Walk up Nanny Lane, looking backwards at the valley views, to the fell path leaving left for Wansfell Pike.*

D Here, there are views which open out suddenly as you climb. If it is clear there is a splendid panoramic view over all the main fells from Coniston Old Man on the left to the High Street range on the right. The highest land, including Scafell, Scafell Pike, Great Gable and Bowfell can be seen a little north of west.

10 Descend slowly with great care *to the lane and turn left.*

11 *Watch for the gate into a wooded ravine containing Stock Ghyll waterfalls.*

E There are several falls, the main one of which is 60ft (18.3m).

12 *Follow the path down by the ghyll side to Ambleside.*

Walk 14
UNDERBARROW AND CUNSWICK SCARS
7 miles (11.3km) 625ft (190.5m) Moderate; some steepness

The main appeal of this walk from Kendal is the view on a clear day which bursts as a visual bombshell as the edge of a limestone precipice is reached. Given the right conditions the whole of the Lake District's central fells are revealed across a lovely green valley far below, with pastures, woodland and hedges, hamlets and farmsteads. No skilful town and country planners laid out this landscape. It evolved naturally. But the walk is also one

for the naturalist, as the ridges of carboniferous limestone, with 'pavements' have the rich distinctive flora. The walk begins by going through a Kendal suburb, which is quiet and pleasant.

1 *Start at Kendal Town Hall. Walk up All Hallows Lane opposite.*

A The obelisk on the left is on the site of what was Kendal's Norman motte and bailey castle, built in 11th century and replaced a century later by the castle on the east of the

town. The obelisk also commemorates the revolution of 1688.

2 *Road junctions. The one on the left goes to the hospital. Take the middle road - Brigsteer Road.*

3 *The road crosses the bridge.*

4 *After passing some stone gateposts on the right seek a stile there (signposted). Cross it and pick up the grassy path across a meadow, through the iron gate in the wall, and on to another stile and straight on.*

B The view to the far fells includes, looking left to right, the Coniston Old Man range some 13 miles (21km) away as the crow flies; Langdale Pikes some 17 miles (27km) distant. Beyond them, the roof of England with Scafell Pike (3210ft/978m) about 20 miles (32km) away. Then there are the fells of Grasmere, Fairfield and Helvellyn (17 miles/27km) before reaching the High Street range. On the extreme left is a view across Morecambe Bay.

5 *The edge of escarpment. Go right and follow the path on the cliff edge.*

C Eccentric monstrosity is the 'mushroom' which once served as an indicator for the view. On the cliff edge discerning botanists will note that the Whitebeam here is *Sorbus Aria var rupicola* a variety which grows here, in Scotland and Scandinavia.

6 *The path joins the road by the kissing-gate. Go right alongside the road.*

7 *Watch for a signed track starting on the left before the house. Go left up it.*

8 *Do **not** go through gate, but turn right just before it to pick up a path going round the wall corner and alongside a walled wood.*

9 *Follow the path on the edge of the escarpment to the cairned summit.*

D Main interest apart from the flora is the view north and north-west.

10 *The path doubles back at a sharp angle. It is not distinct at first on the grass but is more visible further on when it aims for the footbridge over the bypass road.*

11 *There is a stile at the corner. Continue on from it.*

12 *The path continues over the footbridge and goes in a fairly straight line on through stiles ('fatman's agonies'). The path is a little obscured by the golf course mowing but goes on the same line, then bears to the left-hand corner of a large wood.*

13 *From a viewpoint with seats there is a commanding prospect of the town. Join the paths meandering through Serpentine Woods. Eventually any one of them leads to a road and down into Kendal centre.*

Walk 15
ORREST HEAD WALK

2½ miles (4km) Moderate; some wet patches

then go through an iron gate at the end and up to the viewpoint.

A There is a plinth with a view indicator, sometimes alas unreadable through vandalism. Directly and more prominently in front is the Coniston Old Man range (2631ft/801.9m) with the bulky shoulder of Wetherlam to the right. Further right are the humps of Crinkle Crags with Pike O'Blisco in the foreground. Beyond, continuing to the right, is the Scafell range, with its highest point Scafell Pike (3210ft/978m); nearer is Bowfell (2960ft/902.2m) and Esk Pike to the right again. Beyond is Great End, the northern hump of the Scafell range. The Pikes of Langdale are readily recognisable, as are the ridges of High Raise and Ullscarf. Look to the north-west and see the Fairfield range, with Wansfell, above Ambleside in front. To the north-east is the High Street range. Further east are the Yorkshire Hills.

There is an excellent view of the lake, with the woodland facing Claife Heights. The lake appears to be shorter than it is as Belle Isle looks like a southern shoreline.

4 Walk on north on a path from the summit. This crosses fields towards a distant roadway. Wet areas can be avoided with care.

5 Cross the stile on to a minor road. Turn left down it.

6 Keep left on a surfaced road. Join the major road and turn left to walk a short distance.

7 Go through the iron gate on to a track.

8 Follow the track and path to starting point.

Orrest Head is a short walk from Windermere Town, yet it is one of the most rewarding viewpoints in the district, giving an astonishing panorama of the central mountains. It is best done on a clear day. The walk goes beyond the Head across the fields and back through the woods of Elleray Bank.

1 The walk starts from the north side of

the A591 almost opposite to its junction with the road down to Bowness and the railway station approach. It begins up a tarmacadam lane.

2 Follow the tarmacadam lane as far as it goes. It turns into an unsurfaced track to a terrace with a seat (good viewpoint for the lake) then into a path going over tree roots by a wall.

3 A track is reached, go right with it,

32